THE STORY OF JOB

THE STORY

Retold and Illustrated

OF JOB

by **Beverly Brodsky**

George Braziller   **New York**

I would like to thank Julia Ballerini, Ya'aqov Berman, Lois Borgenicht, Hannah Frasinelli, Alexandra Johnson, Joseph Katz and Friends, Joy Kestenbaum, Monica Werblud, and especially Yoshiaki Yoshinari for their support and insight during various stages of this endeavor.

I would also like to express my deepest gratitude to Beatrice Rehl, Editor, and Cynthia Hollandsworth, Art Director, of George Braziller, Inc.

Beverly Brodsky
Artist/Author

Published in the United States in 1986 by George Braziller, Inc.

George Braziller, Inc.
One Park Avenue
New York, New York 10016

First edition

Library of Congress Cataloguing in Publication data:

Brodsky, Beverly.
    The story of Job.

    Summary: God tests Job's faith by letting terrible misfortunes befall him.
        1. Job (Biblical figure)—Juvenile literature.
2. Bible. O.T. Job—Biography—Juvenile literature.
3. Bible stories, English—O.T. Job. [1. Job
(Biblical figure) 2. Bible stories—O.T.]
I. Title.
BS580.J5B76 1986   233'.109505   85-24303
ISBN 0-8076-1142-5 (lib. bdg.)

Printed and bound in Milan, Italy by Sagdos, S.p.A.

A Book of Hope

I know a man whose name
is Job who lives in the land of
Uz. He is old and very wise. His eyes
are filled with light. He speaks of mysteries
beyond my understanding. Yet, when he tells his story,
he seems far away and almost sad. His tale is
told to me to share with everyone.
This is Job's story.

One day when God gathered all the divine beings in heaven, Satan, his seven-winged angel, was among them. He was called the Wicked One, because he was a troublemaker. God asked him: "Where have you been?" And the Wicked One answered, "I have been sailing over the land and walking on it, also." Then the Lord said to him, "Have you seen My servant Job? There is no one like him on all the earth. He is blameless and upright and faithful to God. Neither has he sinned." The Wicked One, who had a grudge against all human creation, was especially jealous of Job. He answered God, "Why should Job fear You when You have given him everything: a good wife, many children, animals in abundance, and acres of fertile land to sow. No man is wealthier than Job himself. Take everything away from him, his fortunes and all his blessings, and You will see that he will no longer love You. He will curse You to Your face." And God allowed the Wicked One to go to earth to destroy everything Job had.

In Uz, Job's servants came to him. One by one they
brought him sad tidings.
    "A fire killed your sheep!"
    "An army slaughtered your camels!"
    "A great wind crushed your son's house
     and killed your children!"

Job and his wife mourned. Job tore away
his robes, cut off his hair, and fell upon
the ground and worshipped. He
chanted, "The Lord has given,
and the Lord has taken
away; blessed be the
name of the Lord."

In spite of everything
that had happened,
Job did not curse God.
At this, the Wicked One grew
angrier and more jealous. When
called by God the second time, he said,
"You have allowed me to take away all Job's
possessions and his blessings. See what happens
if You let me take away his health. He will surely
curse You then." And God said to the Wicked One, "Job
is in your power. Only, spare his life." The Wicked One agreed.
He left the company of God and all the angels in heaven and flew to earth.

When the sun rose in the morning, Job's body was transformed. His flesh ached all over. He was covered with dust and ashes. His beautiful robes turned into rags. He withered like the garden and the fields. Job's wife came to him. She tried to feed and comfort him. And when he could no longer be nourished or comforted, she told him, "Curse God so that you will die." Job answered, "What, should we receive only the blessings from God and should we not receive the misfortunes as well?" Job's wife was astonished. Then she was sorrowful. She felt that there was nothing more she could do.

After awhile Job's friends heard about his misfortunes. They traveled from far away lands to see and comfort him. When Eliphaz the Temanite, Bildad the Shuhite, and Zophar the Naamathite saw Job, they did not recognize him and so they wept. They tore their robes, sprinkled dust upon their heads, and sat down in silence for seven days and seven nights. When Job spoke, his words were full of pain. He complained against God who was silent. Why didn't God hear him when he needed Him most? "Perish the day on which I was born. May that day turn to darkness," Job cried. Still, he did not curse God.

Job's friends were disturbed by his bitter complaints. They blamed him. "It is your fault, Job," said Eliphaz. "You must have done something wicked. Trouble doesn't just spring from the ground. Those that do wicked deeds will have wicked things happen to them. And Bildad spoke, too, saying, "All that is wicked is being punished, and all that is punished is wicked. Ask God's forgiveness. Surely He would not harm a blameless man. If you are innocent, He will protect you."

Job replied, "Pity me! You are my friends. You misjudge me. Your words are empty as the wind. I know I am not perfect. It wasn't meant to be. Don't you see that I have not wronged? I have saved the poor, fed the hungry, and guided the ignorant. I became eyes to the blind and feet to the lame. I protected all who came to my door. Those who were lost were never turned away. I love and fear God and pray to Him everyday and with burnt offerings in case my sons might have sinned, as well. I treasure God's words more than bread. If I am wicked, and I do not know it, then it is up to God to tell me to my face and judge me now. After all, am I not His handiwork?"

Then Job said to his friends, "I feel alone. You turned from me. You did not comfort me. Bring me into the desert and place me beneath a tree. I will remain there until I find God." And Job's friends did as he had asked.

Job looked to the
east to find God. He
wasn't there. Job looked
to the west. Still, he did not
see Him. North and south
as well. Still, He was
hidden. Where was
He? Where was
His guidance
now?

Suddenly, a great storm blackened the sky. And the Lord God replied
to Job from out of the whirlwind and said, "Job, who are these
friends of yours who advise you? They are unwise. They
speak without understanding and true knowledge of
Me. Stand up like a mighty man and listen
to My questions. Answer Me."

"Where were you when I laid the foundations of the earth
and created the laws of the heavens? You were not
yet born. I had not even made you. Have
you ever commanded the day to break?
Who gave the dawn its radiance?"

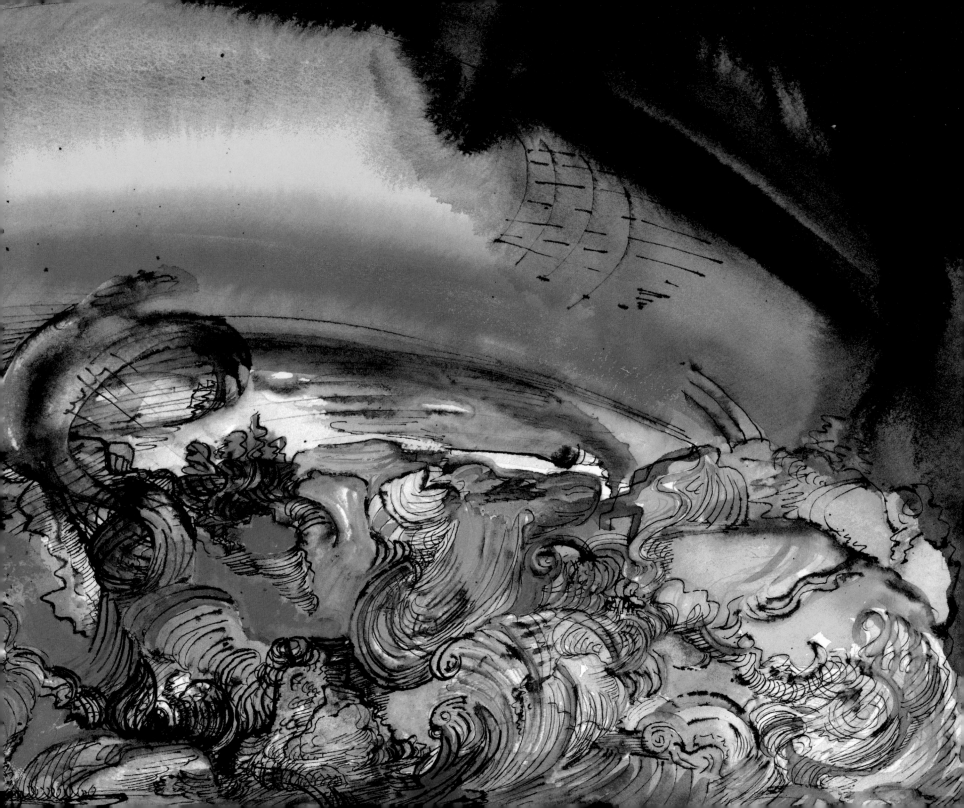

Can you cause the rain to cover the wasteland
so that blades of grass spring forth? Who
gave understanding to the mind? Is
it by your wisdom that the hawk
spreads its wings and
flies south?

Who gave the
horse its strength?

Does the eagle soar at your
command, building its nest
high upon a rock? Since
you complain against God
and His ways and want to
be judged, you must reply."

Job was weak. But he moved slowly to his feet and looked at the whirlwind and in a whisper said, "I am so small compared to the universe and my knowledge of You is so little. What can I say? What do you expect of me?" Job trembled and clapped his hand to his mouth.

Again, God's voice thundered from within the storm. "Stand up like a mighty man and speak out. Do you question My justice and complain against Me so that you may be the one who is right? Can *you* manage the order in the universe? Can *you* deliver the righteous and remove the wickedness in the world? If you can then you are greater than I and I will admit to you that you can save yourself with your own right hand."

Once again, Job pulled himself up and replied, "I know that You can do everything and that You know everything. I know that all things made by You are mysteries. Who can hope to know Your secret? Who can hope to find You and the living source of Your wisdom?" Job looked up at the whirlwind and replied once more, "My heart is open. My soul sings out to you. I heard You with my ears and now I see You, from deep within, and with my eyes."

At that moment, God covered Job all over with the splendor of His radiance.

God summoned Job's friends and commanded them
to offer seven bullocks and seven rams as a burnt
offering to put before Job and they repented.
Afterwards, God commanded Job to
forgive his friends and to pray for
them. And Job did as the
Lord God had commanded.

When Job returned to his house he
found that all his brothers and sisters
and all his friends were there to care for him
and to comfort him. And, because of all his misfortunes
they did the thing that was right. Each and every one
gave Job a gold coin and a gold ring. Then, they sat
down with Job and everyone shared bread with
him and among themselves.

The Lord God
rewarded Job
giving him
twice his fortune.

Job is old
and full of days.